THE LUNGS
AND BREATHING

The Human Body

THE LUNGS AND BREATHING

Brian R. Ward

Series consultant:
Dr A. R. Maryon-Davis
MB, BChir, MSc, MRCS, MRCP

The Human Body

Franklin Watts
London New York Sydney Toronto

First published in Great Britain 1982
Franklin Watts Limited
8 Cork Street
London W1

First published in the United States of America 1982
Franklin Watts Inc.
730 Fifth Avenue
New York, N.Y. 10019

UK edition: ISBN 0 85166 946 8
US edition: ISBN 0-531-04358-4
Library of Congress Catalog Card No: 81-51680

Designed by Howard Dyke

Phototypeset by Computape (Pickering) Ltd, North Yorkshire
Printed in Great Britain by E. T. Heron, London and Essex

Acknowledgments

The illustrations were prepared by: Andrew Aloof, Marion
Appleton, Howard Dyke, David Holmes, David Mallot,
Charles Raymond.

Contents

Introduction

All the **cells** of the body need **oxygen** so that they can live and grow. This colorless gas is present in the air we breathe, and it is the function of the lungs to extract oxygen from the air, and to transfer it to the blood where it can be carried to the cells of the body.

Living cells produce **carbon dioxide**, another colorless gas, as a waste product. The lungs remove this gas from the blood before it can build up to harmful levels.

The passage of air in and out of the **lungs** also serves other important functions. Air passing through the nose allows us to have a sense of smell, and also takes part in the sensation of taste.

We also use the air currents in the throat to generate sound, so that we can talk.

Yet another function of breathing is to regulate the amount of water present in the system and to help cool the body.

The whole breathing apparatus, or **respiratory system**, is one of the main life-support systems of the body. Its structure consists of a pair of sponge-like lungs in the chest, supplied by branching air pipes connecting with the mouth and nose. The lungs have a very large blood supply, and nearly half of the heart's blood output is pumped to the lungs to collect oxygen.

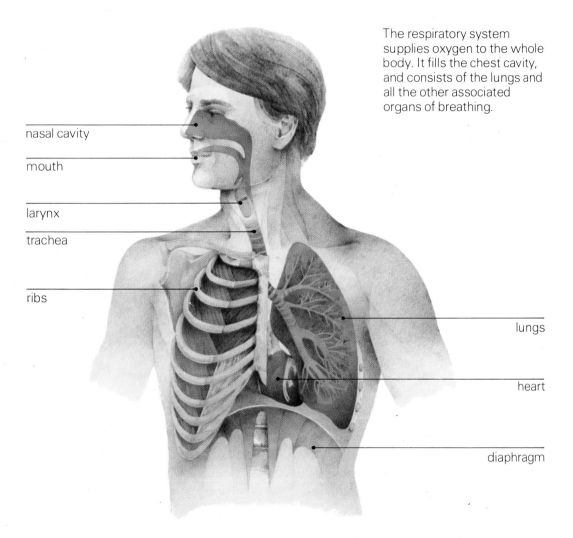

The respiratory system supplies oxygen to the whole body. It fills the chest cavity, and consists of the lungs and all the other associated organs of breathing.

nasal cavity

mouth

larynx

trachea

ribs

lungs

heart

diaphragm

7

The lungs

The lungs are large, spongy organs in the upper chest. Air enters and leaves the lungs through a system of bronchial airways.

We have two lungs: large spongy organs located in the chest cavity. They are of slightly different sizes and shapes. The right lung is the larger, and is divided into three separate parts. The smaller left lung is in two sections. In an adult, the two lungs together weigh about $2\frac{1}{2}$ lb (1 kg).

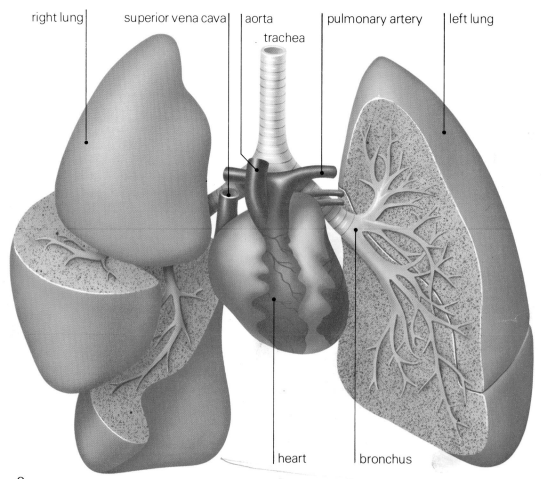

right lung | superior vena cava | aorta | pulmonary artery | left lung

trachea

heart | bronchus

The lungs themselves and the inside of the chest wall are covered with a thin, slippery membrane called the **pleura**. This lets the lungs move about slightly as we breathe, sliding without causing damage. The heart fits closely between the lungs near the center of the chest cavity, and its pumping movements against the lungs are also lubricated by the pleura.

The lungs are pale pink in color in a newborn baby, but they become darker throughout life. This is due to impurities in the air we inhale, some of which cannot be removed and which gradually darken the lungs.

Before strict industrial health laws existed, the lungs of miners and quarrymen, after a lifetime of inhaling dust, could become completely hard and stonelike. Only in people like Eskimos, living in a dust-free atmosphere, do lungs remain pink throughout life.

Lungs are among the last organs to develop properly in an unborn baby, and this is the cause of breathing problems which often affect babies born prematurely.

The lungs of a newborn child are delicate pink. They darken throughout life, and in a miner, who inhales dust for many years, the lungs may become hard and blackened.

child's lung

miner's lung

The nose and mouth

We can breathe equally well through nose or mouth, although most of the time we breathe through the nose only. Breathing through the mouth is useful when we need extra air during exercise like running.

Air normally enters the paired nostrils and passes into a large space called the nasal cavity. This is divided into smaller areas by thin shelves of bone called **nasal conchae**, or **turbinates**. The whole nasal cavity is lined with a thin, moist sheet of **mucous membrane**, and has a very large blood supply. The nasal cavity serves to clean the air we breathe, as large inhaled particles stick to the mucous membrane. Here, too, cold air is warmed before passing to the lungs. A patch of special tissue detects odors present in the air.

More air spaces called **sinuses** open into the nasal cavity. These sometimes become inflamed and blocked, causing **sinusitis**.

Air leaves the nasal cavity and enters the **pharynx**, or throat, on its way to the lungs. A flap called the **uvula**, at the back of the soft **palate**, can seal off the nasal cavity or the airway through the mouth, according to need.

The mouth and throat have a complicated structure to allow them to carry out several functions. They are involved in breathing, chewing, swallowing, voice production and several other body processes.

The lips and tongue play no direct part in breathing, except in aiding the uvula to shut off the air flow through the mouth under some circumstances. Snoring is caused by air forcing its way past the uvula when a sleeping person breathes partly through the mouth.

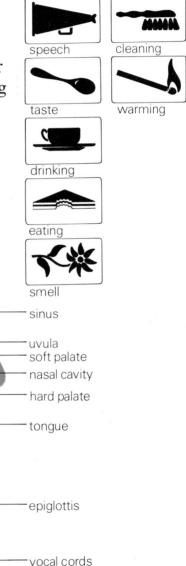

speech

cleaning

taste

warming

drinking

eating

smell

sinus

uvula

soft palate

nasal cavity

hard palate

tongue

epiglottis

vocal cords

trachea

esophagus

Airways to the lungs

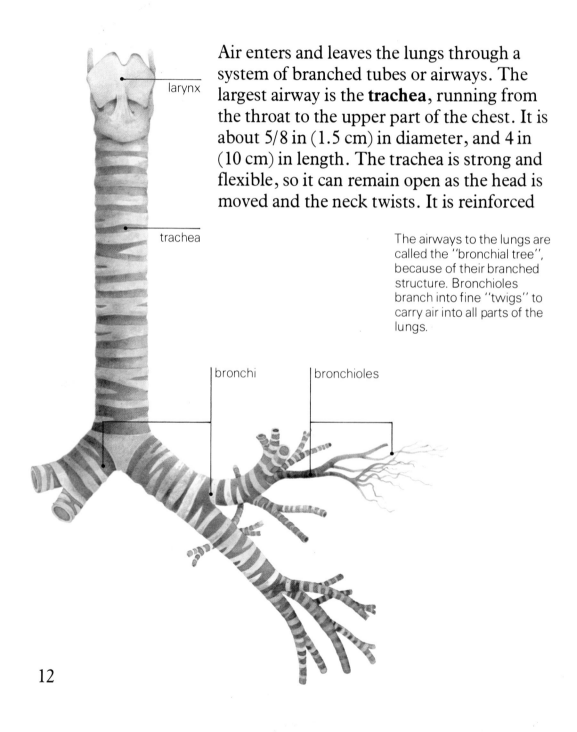

larynx

trachea

bronchi

bronchioles

Air enters and leaves the lungs through a system of branched tubes or airways. The largest airway is the **trachea**, running from the throat to the upper part of the chest. It is about 5/8 in (1.5 cm) in diameter, and 4 in (10 cm) in length. The trachea is strong and flexible, so it can remain open as the head is moved and the neck twists. It is reinforced

The airways to the lungs are called the "bronchial tree", because of their branched structure. Bronchioles branch into fine "twigs" to carry air into all parts of the lungs.

along its length by many horseshoe-shaped sections of **cartilage**, a tough, rubbery material. The trachea is pressed tightly against the **esophagus**, through which food passes to the stomach.

In the upper chest the trachea branches into left and right **bronchi**. These are similarly reinforced, short tubes which enter the lungs. Here they branch again and again, into **bronchioles**, which spread through the lungs like twigs on a tree. The smallest bronchioles are about 1/25 in (1 mm) in diameter. They differ from the larger airways in having no cartilage to support their walls. Instead, they have strands of smooth muscle wound around them. These can contract to narrow the tubular bronchioles and restrict the flow of air. The whole "bronchial tree" of trachea, bronchi and bronchioles is lined with moist mucous membrane. In the lining of the larger airways are **goblet cells**, which produce **mucus** to keep the surface moist, and hair-like **cilia**, which help to keep the system clean.

cartilage   esophagus

The trachea is supported by horseshoe-shaped pieces of cartilage. The esophagus lies against the open end of the cartilage.

The diaphragm

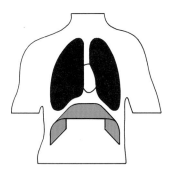

The diaphragm is a dome-shaped sheet of muscle positioned just below the lungs.

The lungs fill the chest cavity formed by the rib cage. The ribs protect the heart and lungs from damage, and are important in breathing.

The floor of the chest cavity is formed by the **diaphragm**. This is a strong sheet made up from criss-crossed layers of muscle, and separates the contents of the chest – the heart and lungs – from the organs in the abdomen. The stomach and liver fit just below the diaphragm. Large blood vessels such as the **aorta** and **vena cava** pass through the diaphragm, together with the esophagus.

At the front of the body, the diaphragm follows the curved line of the bottom of the rib cage. Deeper in the chest, it curves even more, into a bell shape. Tough supporting **ligaments** help to keep the diaphragm curved when its muscles are relaxed.

When the diaphragm muscles shorten, or contract, the diaphragm flattens and moves lower in the chest. This is the basis of normal quiet breathing.

Nerves supplying the diaphragm and other organs in the abdomen are spread out just below the ribs. If we are struck violently in the abdomen, the action of these nerves is temporarily affected, and the diaphragm tenses, or goes into a spasm. This is commonly called "winding."

A violent blow to the stomach can temporarily affect the nerves which cause the diaphragm to contract. For a short time, breathing becomes very difficult. This is known as being "winded."

15

The chest

The chest is given its shape by the rib cage. Ribs are flat bones, hinged at the spine, that curve around to the front of the chest. Here most are attached to the **sternum**, or breastbone, a long, flat bone to which ribs are connected by a flexible joint of cartilage.

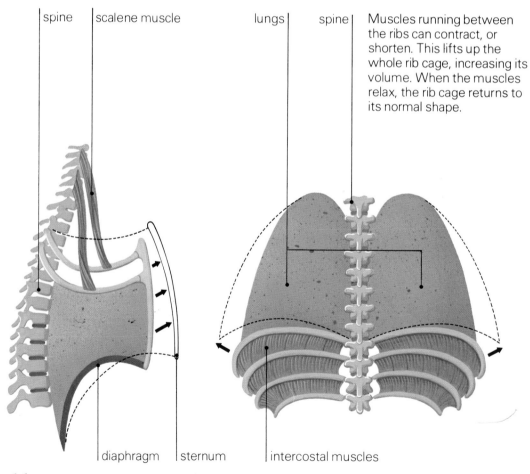

spine   scalene muscle   lungs   spine

Muscles running between the ribs can contract, or shorten. This lifts up the whole rib cage, increasing its volume. When the muscles relax, the rib cage returns to its normal shape.

diaphragm   sternum   intercostal muscles

The lower ribs have their tips connected by cartilage to the ribs above. The last two hang free and are known as "floating ribs."

This structure produces a rib cage which is immensely strong. At the same time, this strong cage is capable of movement. Unlike most other bones, ribs are very flexible and springy.

All the ribs are joined to the spine, and nearly all are attached to the sternum or to each other in such a way that they can all be moved together, as the sternum is raised up and outward. This increases the volume of the rib cage.

Between each set of ribs run two sheets of **intercostal muscles** which, as they contract, pull each rib closer to the next. This has the effect of raising the whole rib cage. As the muscles relax, the rib cage drops back down to its normal position, and regains its original volume.

How we breathe

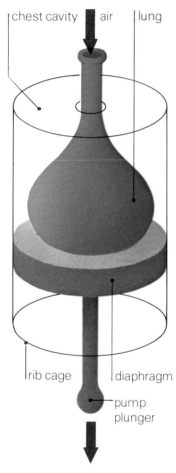

chest cavity   air   lung

rib cage   diaphragm

pump
plunger

The respiratory system
works like a simple air pump,
with the diaphragm acting as
the plunger, and the rib cage
acting as the outer casing.

Normal quiet breathing is carried out by movement of the diaphragm. As it contracts, the diaphragm flattens out, increasing the volume of the chest cavity. Air rushes into the lungs to fill this extra space. In quiet breathing, the diaphragm moves down only about 5/8 in (1.5 cm), but in deep breathing it may move as much as 3 in (7.5 cm).

Breathing works like a bellows, or a water pump, relying on the pressure of the air around us to push air into the lungs as the volume of the chest cavity enlarges.

When the diaphragm relaxes, it regains its former domed shape, and the lungs are squeezed slightly, forcing the remaining air out again.

This quiet diaphragmic breathing is the usual method of breathing, when the chest can hardly be seen to rise and fall. However, the abdomen can be seen moving gently as the diaphragm contracts and relaxes.

When we exert ourselves, the muscles need a greater supply of oxygen from the blood, and the action of the diaphragm alone cannot provide deep enough breathing. The ribs are now used, being moved by the intercostal muscles to produce a much larger expansion and contraction of the chest, and with it, the lungs.

In diaphragmic breathing, air enters the lungs as the diaphragm contracts, becoming more flattened. When it resumes its relaxed domed shape, air is forced out of the lungs again.

When the chest is used for deep breathing, muscles raise the rib cage to increase its volume. This causes air to rush into the lungs. Air is forced out when the muscles relax.

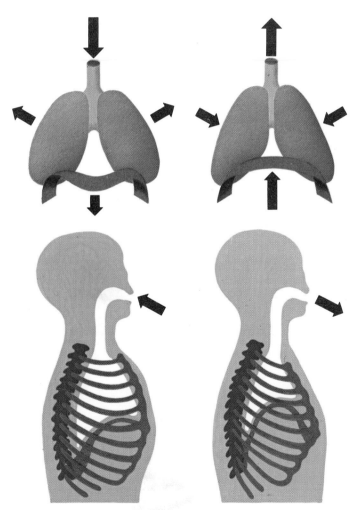

The air we breathe

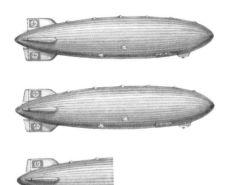

During a lifetime, we breathe a volume of air equal to the capacity of 2½ enormous airships.

The amount of air we breathe varies depending on our activity. When resting, an adult breathes about 1 pint of air with each breath. We normally breathe about 10 to 14 times each minute, making our air intake 10 to 14 pints per minute.

But if we do vigorous exercise, such as running, the air intake leaps to as much as 210 pints per minute, to supply extra oxygen to the muscles. Even so, within a few minutes all the spare oxygen in the blood will have been used, and we continue panting for a while even after the exertion has finished.

Each day we breathe about 500 cubic ft of air, and in an entire lifetime, nearly 14,000,000 cubic ft – enough to fill 2½ enormous airships, or a good-sized oil tanker.

We seldom completely fill our lungs during breathing, and we never completely empty them. Even after breathing out as hard as possible, there remain about 3 pints of air in the lungs, called the **residual volume**. The waste gas, carbon dioxide, tends to accumulate in this residual volume. The deep breathing of athletes *before* taking exercise flushes all this carbon dioxide from their lungs, replacing it with oxygen.

Only a small volume of air moves in and out of the lungs during normal breathing.

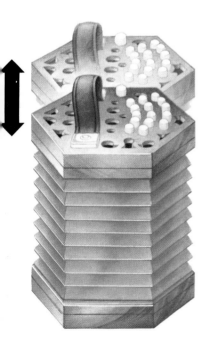

During vigorous exercise the lungs are filled to their greatest extent.

Even when we breathe out forcibly, some air remains in the lungs.

Oxygen in the lungs

The surface area of the alveoli in the lungs has been compared to the area of a tennis court.

At the ends of the smallest bronchioles are clusters of tiny air sacs called **alveoli**, where oxygen is absorbed and carbon dioxide is released. There are more than 300 million of these alveoli in an adult's lungs, and together they have a huge surface area of 95 sq yd (80 sq m), or more than 40 times the whole surface area of the skin.

Alveoli have thin walls, only one cell thick, and these walls contain a network of fine **capillaries** that carry blood. Air which is rich in oxygen and which contains little carbon dioxide enters the alveoli. The oxygen passes freely through the walls of the alveoli and the capillaries and enters the red blood cells. Here the oxygen combines loosely with a red substance called **hemoglobin**, to form **oxyhemoglobin**. The red cells move on in the bloodstream, now carrying oxygen which will be given up to other body cells as needed.

Dissolved in the clear blood **plasma** in which red cells float is the waste gas carbon dioxide, produced by all the cells of the body. This passes out into the alveoli, and is flushed out of the lungs when we breathe out. Excess water is also produced by some chemical reactions in the body, and this evaporates into the air leaving the lungs.

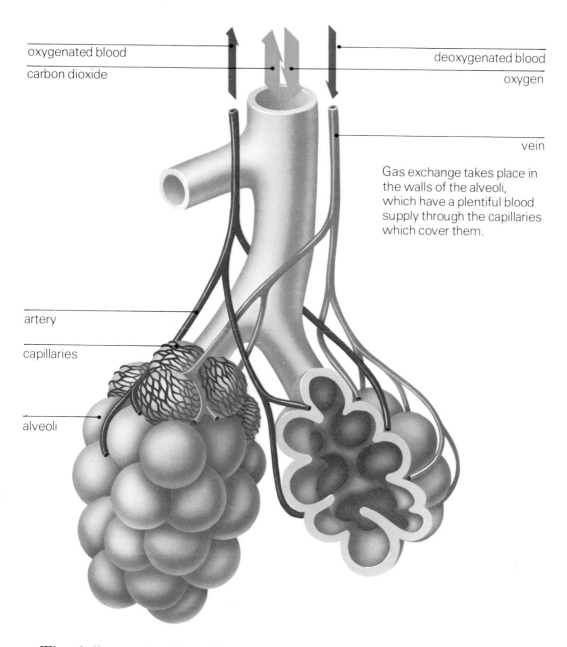

oxygenated blood

carbon dioxide

deoxygenated blood

oxygen

vein

Gas exchange takes place in
the walls of the alveoli,
which have a plentiful blood
supply through the capillaries
which cover them.

artery

capillaries

alveoli

The delicate alveoli walls are covered with
a chemical which acts as a "non-stick"
coating to prevent the air sacs from sticking
to each other and collapsing. This also
lubricates the alveoli and reduces the effort
needed for breathing.

Blood circulation to the lungs

It would be wasteful if oxygenated blood were to become mixed with blood from which oxygen had already been used by the body. To avoid this situation, blood is circulated in two stages.

The heart itself is divided into two parts, each pumping the blood to a different part of the body. The left side of the heart is the more powerful, pumping oxygenated blood all around the body, through a huge network of arteries and capillaries. As the blood passes through the capillaries, it gives up its oxygen and takes in carbon dioxide and water. Now it is deoxygenated blood, which returns along veins to the right side of the heart.

From the smaller, right side of the heart, blood is pumped directly to the lungs, through arteries and then through capillaries in the lungs, where it picks up oxygen and loses its dissolved carbon dioxide and water. The oxygenated blood now returns to the left side of the heart to be pumped around the body, repeating the cycle again.

In this way oxygenated and deoxygenated blood are kept quite separate in the circulation. Fresh oxygen is continually brought in through the lungs, and waste carbon dioxide and water are eliminated as fast as they are produced.

This simplified diagram
shows how blood circulates
around the body, carrying
oxygen supplies to the
tissues and replenishing its
oxygen in the lungs.

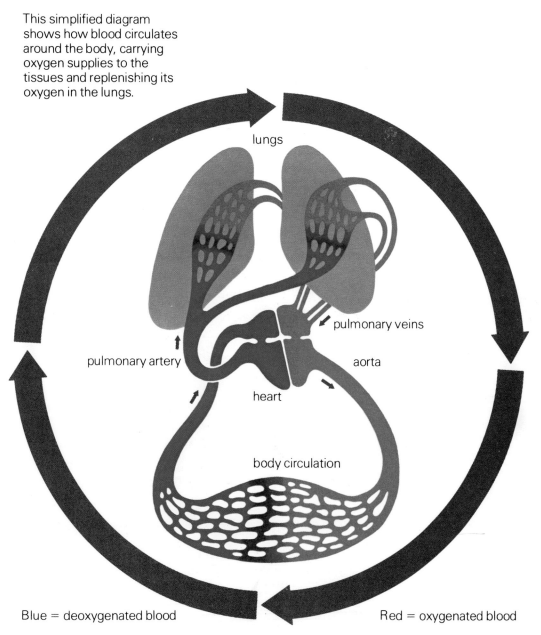

lungs

pulmonary veins

pulmonary artery

aorta

heart

body circulation

Blue = deoxygenated blood

Red = oxygenated blood

Gas transfer in the tissues

Capillaries containing oxygenated blood penetrate almost every part of the body. The only living cells which do not have a blood supply are in parts of the eye, where blood would block vision. These cells must absorb their oxygen directly from the surrounding air.

All other cells are supplied with the oxygen locked up in the red cells as oxyhemoglobin, a bright red pigment.

Capillaries are never far from living cells, branching and twining through muscles, nerves and all other types of tissue. Oxygen splits off from the oxyhemoglobin and enters the cells. Here it reacts with chemicals already in the cell to produce energy which may be used by the cells or stored for later use as a reserve power supply. The same reaction produces carbon dioxide and water, which pass out of the cell into the blood.

The blood continues on its way, the red cells now containing only hemoglobin, which is dark purplish-red, and dissolved carbon dioxide, together with water.

This chemical process of the exchange of oxygen for carbon dioxide and water is called **respiration**, and it is one of the most important functions of any living organism.

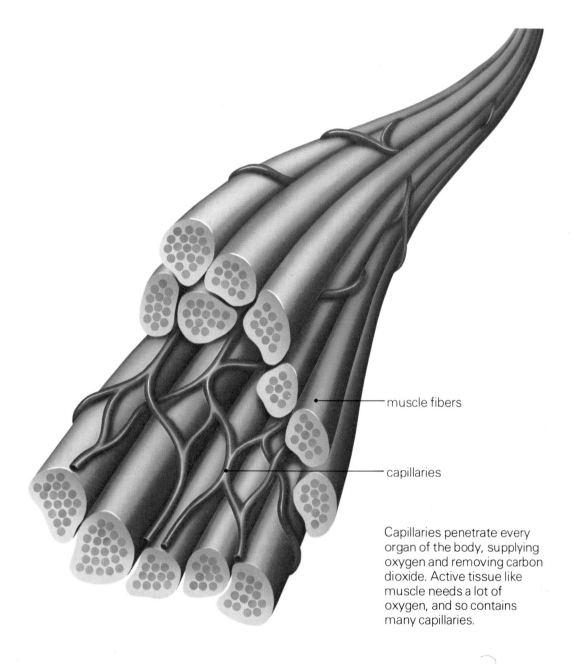

muscle fibers

capillaries

Capillaries penetrate every organ of the body, supplying oxygen and removing carbon dioxide. Active tissue like muscle needs a lot of oxygen, and so contains many capillaries.

Parts of the body having a high energy requirement need a greater blood supply. For this reason the brain and muscles all have very large blood supplies, and are penetrated by large numbers of capillaries.

27

What makes us breathe?

Many factors control our rate of breathing. The body continuously measures its need for oxygen and monitors the building up of waste carbon dioxide. The brain then issues "instructions" to the organs of breathing so the required changes can be made.

● breathing control center in the brain
1 carotid body, measures oxygen level in the blood
2 lungs
3 carbon dioxide level is measured in the blood
4 diaphragm

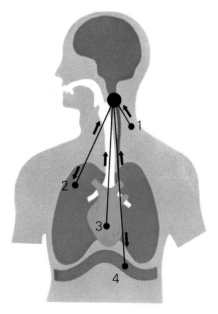

Breathing is completely automatic. It continues through consciousness and sleep without our having to make any active breathing effort. We can vary the rate of breathing, as usually happens when we stop to think about it, and we can consciously breathe more deeply. What we cannot do is to stop breathing altogether for much more than a minute.

If the breath is held for long enough, automatic mechanisms in the body take over, and it becomes impossible to avoid taking a deep breath.

A part of the brain which controls all our important body functions automatically sends nerve impulses down the spinal cord to the diaphragm and the intercostal muscles, instructing them to contract regularly. We can override these instructions, but only for a short while.

The rate and depth of breathing is also controlled chemically. During exertion, muscles increase their production of waste carbon dioxide, which begins to build up in the blood. The control center in the brain detects this increase in carbon dioxide and steps up the rate and depth of breathing to flush out the unwanted dissolved gas through the lungs.

Yet another similar mechanism measures the oxygen level of the blood through a chemical detector in the side of the neck. This detector passes nerve instructions to the brain to speed up or slow down the rate of breathing.

The body's need for oxygen is much reduced during sleep. The brain maintains breathing at a slower and shallower level.

The voice box

All the air entering and leaving the lungs passes through the **larynx**, or voice box. This is made up of tough cartilage and is positioned at the top of the trachea. You can see the larynx as the bulging "Adam's apple" in the front of the neck.

One important function of the larynx is the production of sound, and the larynx is the basis of the human voice.

The larynx is a tubular box, fitted at the top of the trachea. Across its hollow center are stretched two leathery sheets, the **vocal cords**, with a small triangular gap between them. Several muscles control the tension on these vocal cords. When the muscles contract, the cords are brought closer

In normal breathing, the vocal cords move apart to allow air to flow freely between them.

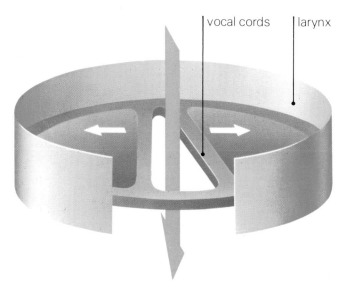

vocal cords | larynx

together, narrowing or closing the gap.

All the air we breathe rushes between the vocal cords. When they are brought closer together, with only a slit between them, they vibrate in the rush of air, exactly like the reed in a clarinet or an organ. This generates sound.

The tighter the vocal cords are stretched, the more shrill is the sound produced. Loudness depends on the amount of air being forced between them.

The quality of the sound produced is affected by resonance, or echoing, in the mouth, nasal cavity, sinuses and chest. This is why blocked sinuses or a cold cause the voice to sound muffled and distorted.

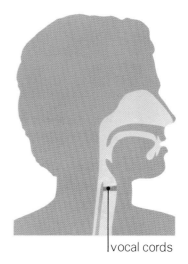

vocal cords

The larynx, or "Adam's apple," containing the vocal cords, is positioned at the front of the throat.

In voice production the vocal cords move together to produce a slit through which air is forced.

The human voice

The larynx can produce sounds as air rushes over the vocal cords. Speech requires that the sounds are altered and controlled, linked together and separated. All this requires very complicated actions by many muscles, moving the jaw, tongue, lips, soft palate and cheeks, in addition to sound control in the larynx.

The teeth and the hard palate, the bony roof of the mouth, also play an important part in speech production or articulation.

Different combinations of actions are required to produce each group of sounds.

Stop sounds like "b" and "p" are produced by suddenly blocking the flow of

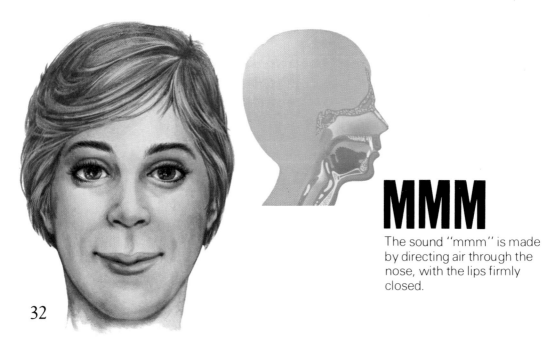

MMM

The sound "mmm" is made by directing air through the nose, with the lips firmly closed.

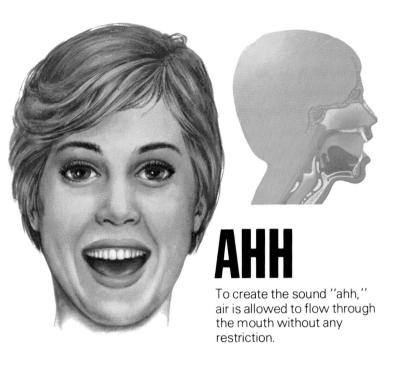

AHH

To create the sound "ahh," air is allowed to flow through the mouth without any restriction.

air with the lips. In "d" and "t," the flow of air is blocked against the hard palate and the teeth; in "g" and "k" it is blocked against the soft palate.

Fricatives are sounds produced by partly blocking the air flow and forcing it through a narrow opening: "v," "f," "s" and "z" are all sounds of this type. To produce vowels, the quality of sound is varied by changing the position of the lips and jaw.

In sounds like "m," "n" and "ng," the air flow is directed through the nasal cavity, and the mouth is closed off.

Some sounds only occur in certain languages and dialects. Examples are the rolled "r" of the Scottish dialect, and the guttural "ch" of German. Other sounds, such as the clicks that form a part of some African languages, are almost impossible to pronounce for those who have not learned to speak the language in childhood.

Swallowing

The opening into the larynx is at the base of the tongue. It is positioned in front of the gullet, or esophagus. This means that air and food must at first share the same passage. A special mechanism is needed to prevent food from passing into the larynx and blocking the trachea, which could cause choking and suffocation.

An automatic action of the larynx prevents food from being inhaled into the lungs.

Food in the mouth is first positioned by the tongue. As it passes back toward the throat, the uvula on the soft palate is raised, blocking off the airway into the nasal cavity, and preventing the food from entering it. The food is then forced into the throat, ready for swallowing.

The larynx is now raised against the base of the tongue, and forced firmly against a small flap called the **epiglottis**, which seals off the airway into the larynx. Touch your throat with your fingers and you will feel this raising of the larynx in your neck, when your "Adam's apple" rises as you swallow.

Food can now pass directly into the esophagus, with no risk of being inhaled, and will be carried down to the stomach by waves of muscular contraction called **peristalsis**.

If, due to hurried swallowing, food does lodge in the larynx, choking may follow, but the food is usually dislodged by coughing. When a very large piece of food is swallowed, you may feel as though you are choking, as the esophagus bulges between the horseshoe-shaped cartilage rings causing the trachea to be partially blocked, and temporarily interfering with the air flow to the lungs.

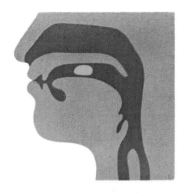

Food is positioned by the tongue, ready for swallowing.

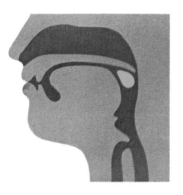

As food enters the back of the mouth, the soft palate closes off the nasal cavity.

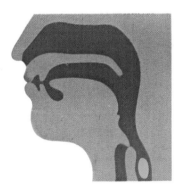

The larynx rises to seal the airway against the epiglottis. Swallowing can now take place safely.

35

Keeping the lungs clean

Even the cleanest air contains dirt particles, and these are deposited on the moist lining of the trachea, bronchi and bronchioles.

There are special mechanisms to clean the lungs of most of this material.

The mucous membrane lining the trachea, bronchi and bronchioles is covered with cilia, which are tiny hair-like structures. Cilia beat back and forth, working together so that their movement is like gusts of wind blowing across a cornfield. Their rowing movement produces a current in the layer of sticky mucus, carrying it steadily toward the trachea together with most of the trapped dirt particles. Dirt trapped in the mucus is shifted out of the lungs at a rate of 3/8 in (1 cm) per minute. When it reaches the throat it is swallowed, and disposed of harmlessly.

Tobacco smoke has a direct effect on this system. It paralyzes the tiny beating cilia, allowing harmful tar to accumulate in the lungs. The tar remains in contact with living cells, rather than being removed quickly by the cilia, as with normal dirt particles.

There are no cilia in the alveoli, and here a different protective mechanism is used. Most dirt particles are trapped in the bronchioles and removed, but those reaching the alveoli are eaten by large, wandering white cells called **macrophages**. These can consume both dirt and bacteria, preventing infection.

Beating cilia propel a layer of sticky mucus out of the lungs, together with the dirt it has collected.

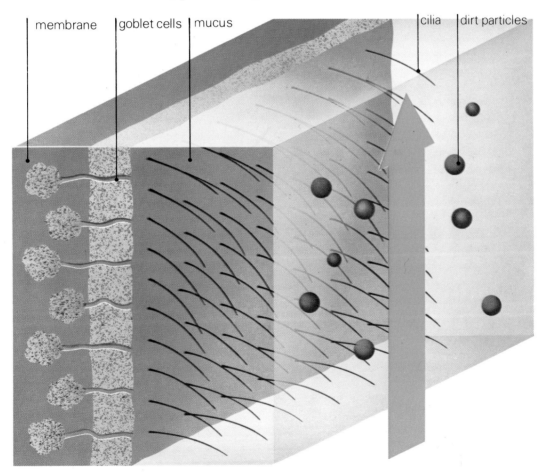

membrane | goblet cells | mucus | cilia | dirt particles

Cleaning the airways

A cough is caused by irritation of the larynx, trachea or bronchi.

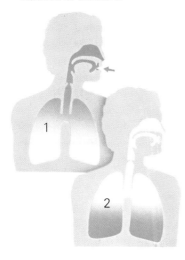

1 A deep breath is inhaled.
2 The vocal cords move together to seal off the airway.

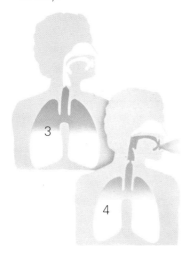

3 Muscles in the chest and abdomen contract to compress the air in the lungs.
4 The vocal cords relax, allowing air to be expelled suddenly through the mouth as a cough.

Some of the ways in which the respiratory system clears itself of blockage or irritation are very obvious. Any attempt by food or other material to enter the air passages is met by an explosive reaction of coughing, which is quite uncontrollable. In a cough, the diaphragm and rib muscles contract violently. The epiglottis closes for a moment, as pressure builds up, and then releases the trapped air with a rush. The air travels out of the trachea at as much as 525 ft (160 m) per second, usually dislodging the obstruction.

In a sneeze, the same explosive expulsion of air takes place, but the tongue blocks the mouth and directs the air through the nose. Here it travels even faster than a cough, with tremendous energy, perhaps even reaching supersonic speed.

Hiccoughs are a disorder of the breathing apparatus, when for no obvious reason the diaphragm contracts sharply. Instead of inhaling in the normal way, the vocal cords slam shut, producing the "hic." Hiccoughs seem to result from an incorrect message being passed along nerves to the diaphragm.

Laughter and crying both result from short, sharp expulsions of breath, while yawning is caused by a deep intake of breath, with the mouth wide open.

38

Sneezing results from irritation of the delicate mucous membrane in the nasal cavity.

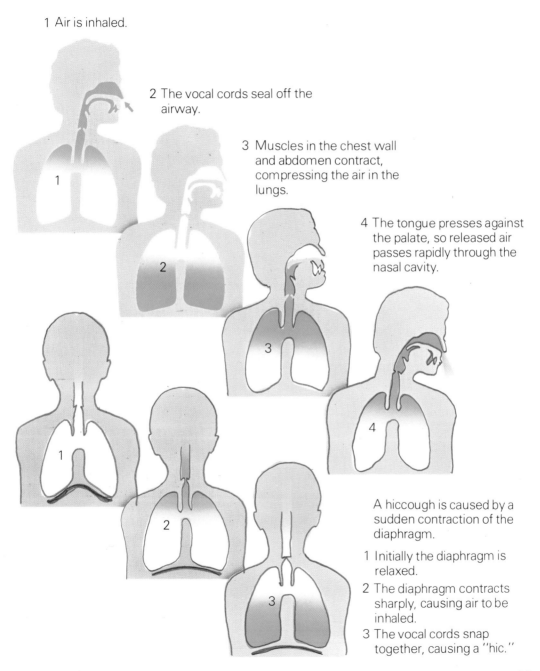

1 Air is inhaled.

2 The vocal cords seal off the airway.

3 Muscles in the chest wall and abdomen contract, compressing the air in the lungs.

4 The tongue presses against the palate, so released air passes rapidly through the nasal cavity.

A hiccough is caused by a sudden contraction of the diaphragm.

1 Initially the diaphragm is relaxed.

2 The diaphragm contracts sharply, causing air to be inhaled.

3 The vocal cords snap together, causing a "hic."

Breathing problems

The respiratory system can be affected by many illnesses, and is particularly prone to bacterial and **virus** infections, as it is in direct contact with germ-laden air.

The viruses of the common cold and influenza enter the body through the nasal passages and lungs, and leave the body the same way to spread the infection. Most common diseases of childhood also enter through the lungs but, unlike colds and influenza, these do not usually cause such noticeable breathing problems.

Tuberculosis is a lung infection caused by a type of bacteria. This disease is now less common in countries with adequate health care.

One of the most common breathing problems is **bronchitis**, caused by inflammation of the bronchi by infection, smoking or some other condition. The bronchi become partly blocked by mucus, causing great difficulty in breathing. **Emphysema** also results in breathing problems, when large areas of the lung cease to work properly, causing oxygen shortage.

Asthma is caused by contraction of the muscle wrapped around the bronchioles, narrowing them and restricting the flow of air. It is sometimes caused by an **allergy**, an

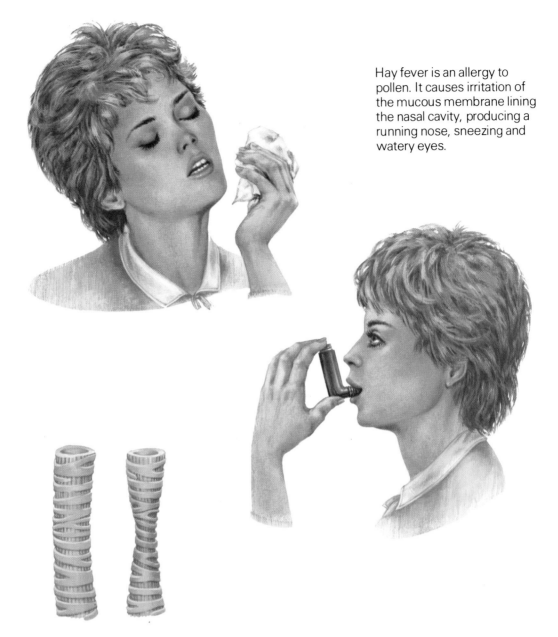

Hay fever is an allergy to pollen. It causes irritation of the mucous membrane lining the nasal cavity, producing a running nose, sneezing and watery eyes.

overreaction by the body's defenses to harmless dust or pollen in the air.

Hay fever is a common allergy causing a runny nose, sneezing, and watery eyes, usually due to a reaction to pollen. It is generally seasonal, depending on which types of pollen are in the air at a particular time of year.

In asthma, muscle wrapped around the bronchioles contracts, narrowing the airway and restricting air flow so it becomes hard to breathe. Special inhalers are used to relieve this condition.

An aquatic existence

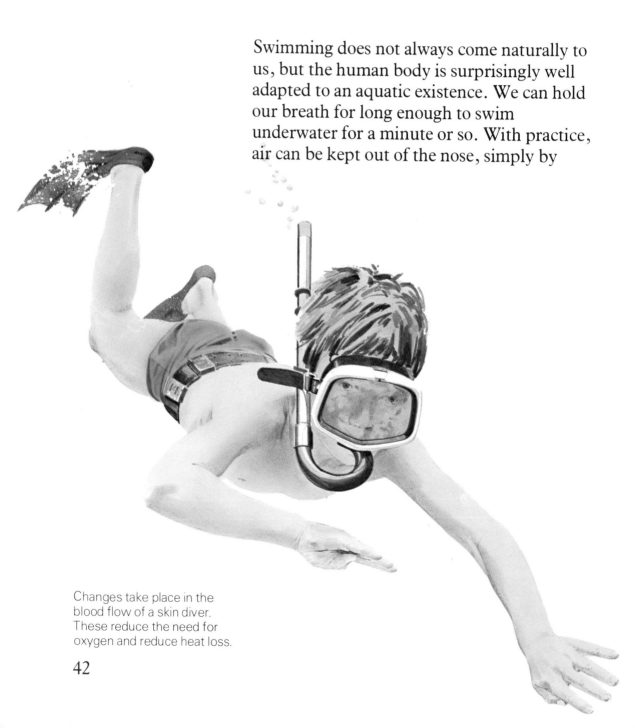

Swimming does not always come naturally to us, but the human body is surprisingly well adapted to an aquatic existence. We can hold our breath for long enough to swim underwater for a minute or so. With practice, air can be kept out of the nose, simply by

Changes take place in the blood flow of a skin diver. These reduce the need for oxygen and reduce heat loss.

blocking off the airway through the nose with the soft palate. The air already in the nasal cavity then prevents the entry of water.

We also possess an unusual mechanism that may be left over from aquatic ancestors. When the face is submerged in cold water, the body directs blood away from the skin and muscles, and increases the blood flow to the internal organs. In this way, the amount of oxygen used is reduced, and heat loss to the water is also reduced. Similar mechanisms exist in ducks, seals, whales and other aquatic warm-blooded birds and mammals.

When we dive deeply, the water presses with great force on the body. A deep-sea diver breathes compressed air at the same pressure as the water outside, so the chest is not crushed, although there may be many tons of water pressure on the body.

At these high pressures, nitrogen as well as oxygen is absorbed from the air through the lungs and dissolves in the bloodstream. If the diver surfaces too quickly after a long dive, the nitrogen can form bubbles in the blood and cause a serious condition called "the bends."

Breathing in high altitudes

With increasing height, the air becomes thinner and there is less oxygen to breathe. Mountain climbers pant more as they reach greater heights, in order to get sufficient oxygen. The summit of Mount Everest is just about the maximum altitude at which it is possible to survive for any length of time.

Aircraft now fly routinely at 33,000 ft (10,000 m) or more, where life would be impossible without artificial oxygen supplies. Modern airliners are pressurized so that the pressure inside their passenger cabins is equivalent to that at about 6,500 ft (2,000 m), which is hardly noticeable to the passengers.

In parts of Africa, Asia and South America, many people live permanently at high altitudes, and in the Andes some live as high as 16,500 ft (5,000 m) above sea level. We would find such life very uncomfortable, but in people born and living under these conditions, body changes have taken place which allow them to remain healthy. Their chests are enlarged to give them greater lung capacity, and their blood contains a much higher proportion of red cells than our own, so it can carry more oxygen. There are disadvantages too, as these barrel-chested South American Indians are very prone to lung disease.

Mountaineers at high altitudes may suffer from lack of oxygen. On very high climbs, artificial oxygen supplies may be needed.

Glossary

Allergy: reaction by the body to harmless substances to which the person has become sensitive. May cause sneezing, runny nose, watery eyes, rashes, itching, etc.

Alveoli: tiny air sacs in the lungs in which oxygen is absorbed from the air and carbon dioxide is removed from the blood.

Aorta: the largest artery in the body, through which all the blood leaving the left side of the heart passes, to be pumped around the body.

Asthma: disease in which the small airways or bronchioles in the lungs become suddenly narrowed, obstructing the air flow. Asthma may be a form of allergy.

Bronchi: pair of airways branching off from the trachea, passing air to the right and left lungs.

Bronchioles: the smallest airways, branching in the lungs and conveying air to the alveoli.

Bronchitis: disease in which the bronchi become inflamed and partly blocked by jelly-like mucus.

Capillaries: the smallest blood vessels. Capillaries penetrate every part of the body, and are important in the exchange of oxygen and carbon dioxide in the lungs.

Carbon dioxide: (CO_2) colorless gas produced by the body as a waste product. CO_2 dissolves in the blood, and is removed in the lungs.

Cartilage: whitish translucent material, which is slightly rubbery. Cartilage cushions joints and is also used to reinforce certain parts of the body.

Cell: smallest unit of the living body. The body is composed of billions of cells, each with its own function.

Cilia: hair-like structures in the mucous membrane which beat back and forth, producing a current in the mucus.

Diaphragm: tough sheet of muscle separating the organs of the chest from those in the abdomen. The diaphragm plays an important part in breathing.

Emphysema: lung disease in which the alveoli are damaged and no longer function properly, reducing the capacity of the lungs to absorb oxygen.

Epiglottis: small flap in the back of the throat which can close to block off the entrance to the larynx, preventing food from entering the airways.

Esophagus: the gullet. Tube through which food is conveyed from the mouth to the stomach.

Fricatives: sounds produced during speech, where the air flow through the mouth is partly blocked.

Goblet cells: cup-shaped cells lining the trachea and bronchi (also found elsewhere in the body) which produce sticky mucus.

Hay fever: an allergy mostly affecting the nose and eyes. Pollen in the air causes an allergic reaction in which the nose itches, and the nose and eyes run continuously.

Hemoglobin: dark red pigment carried in red blood cells. Oxygen becomes attached to hemoglobin and is transported to all parts of the body.

Intercostal muscles: sheets of muscles lying between the ribs, and used in deep breathing.

Larynx: the voice box or "Adam's apple." The larynx is made from cartilage, and is positioned on top of the trachea, at the front of the throat.

Ligament: tough, ropy material used to support joints and organs. Ligaments help hold the diaphragm in its relaxed, curved shape.

Lungs: paired spongy organs in the chest, through which oxygen is absorbed and carbon dioxide is removed from the blood.

Macrophages: large white cells which wander through the lungs, keeping them clean by eating bacteria and particles of dirt.

Mucous membrane: thin moist layer covering most of the organs of the body. Mucous membrane lines the trachea, bronchi and bronchioles.

Mucus: sticky liquid secreted from goblet cells in the mucous membrane, in which dirt particles become stuck and can be removed. Mucus also acts as a protecting film and lubricant.

Nasal conchae: (or turbinates) thin ledges of bone in the nasal cavity which are covered with mucous membrane. These help to clean and warm incoming air.

Oxygen: colorless gas present in the air, needed by every cell in the body. Oxygen is absorbed through the lungs into the blood.

Oxyhemoglobin: substance formed when oxygen becomes attached to hemoglobin in the blood. Oxyhemoglobin is bright red.

Palate: roof of the mouth, divided into the hard and soft palate.

Peristalsis: wave-like muscular movement which pushes food along the digestive system.

Pharynx: the throat passage through which both food and air travel.

Plasma: clear fluid in which red and white blood cells float.

Pleura: thin membrane that forms a protective covering over the lungs and lines the chest cavity.

Residual volume: volume of air still remaining in the lungs after breathing out.

Respiration: chemical process in which living cells use oxygen as a source of energy, releasing carbon dioxide as a waste product.

Respiratory system: mouth, nose, pharynx, larynx, trachea, bronchi, lungs, diaphragm and intercostal muscles. The whole system is used in breathing.

Sinuses: air spaces leading off from the nasal cavity in the cheeks and forehead.

Sinusitis: painful blockage of the sinuses, usually caused by an infection such as a cold.

Sternum: the breastbone, to which most of the ribs are attached at the front of the chest.

Trachea: the largest airway. A short, flexible tube beginning at the larynx and supported by sections of cartilage. From it the two bronchi branch.

Turbinates: *see* Nasal conchae.

Uvula: soft flap at the back of the soft palate, which can seal off the airway into the nasal cavity or the airway through the mouth.

Vena cava: the superior and inferior venae cavae are the largest veins in the body, bringing blood into the heart.

Virus: disease-producing organism which lives inside a cell, which it then "takes over." The body's defenses cannot then recognize the virus and eliminate it, so the disease can be long-lasting.

Vocal cords: tough flaps positioned across the larynx, which vibrate in the air flow to produce sounds.

Index